SCREWED UP
English

TWISTED TRANSLATIONS OF THE
ENGLISH LANGUAGE FROM AROUND THE WORLD

CHARLIE CROKER

Aadamsmedia
Avon, Massachusetts

Published by
Adams Media, an F+W Publications Company
57 Littlefield Street, Avon, MA 02322. U.S.A.
www.adamsmedia.com

ISBN-13: 978-1-59869-512-0
ISBN-10: 1-59869-512-6

Printed in Canada.

J I H G F E D C B A

Library of Congress Cataloging-in-Publication Data

is available from the publisher.

This publication is designed to provide accurate and authoritative information with regard to the subject matter covered. It is sold with the understanding that the publisher is not engaged in rendering legal, accounting, or other professional advice. If legal advice or other expert assistance is required, the services of a competent professional person should be sought.

—From a Declaration of Principles jointly adopted by a Committee of the American Bar Association and a Committee of Publishers and Associations

Many of the designations used by manufacturers and sellers to distinguish their product are claimed as trademarks. Where those designations appear in this book and Adams Media was aware of a trademark claim, the designations have been printed with initial capital letters.

This book is available at quantity discounts for bulk purchases.

For information, please call 1-800-289-0963.

CONTENTS

ACKNOWLEDGMENTS

I am very grateful to the Hoffnung Partnership for permission to quote several replies from German hotels, which the late Gerard Hoffnung immortalized in his 1958 speech to the Oxford Union. (This is available as a BBC recording, "Hoffnung: A Last Encore.")

Thanks are also due to the following for their intrepid efforts in the name of research: Kerry Duckworth, Nigel Farndale, Norman Geras, Markus Grupp, Marie Gumaelius, Rob Heeley, Chris Hope, Alison Lindsay, John Melbourne, Chris Pavlo and Mark Schuck.

It's customary for authors to conclude their acknowledgements with the disclaimer that any errors which follow are entirely their fault. Please understand why I'm not doing that here.

INTRODUCTION

You're in a far-flung corner of the globe, it's the early hours of the morning and you've just checked into your hotel after an exhausting flight. The prospect of a 7:30 business breakfast is filling you with dread, and you've got a nagging feeling you forgot to pack your toothbrush. Very little seems right with the world. But then you notice a sign in the corner of the bathroom: "Please to bathe inside the tub." Despite your tiredness, you can't help but smile. Yes—you've encountered *Screwed Up English*.

All over the world, from Beijing to Buenos Aires, in hotels and restaurants and taxis and zoos (yes, zoos), these priceless nuggets of verbal mistakes lie in wait, ready to brighten the lives of the jaded voyagers who chance upon them. They are the reward points on our travel loyalty card. They are the treats we earn for enduring mislaid luggage, deep-vein thrombosis, and stony-faced flight attendants. Never failing to amuse, they put a spring in our step with nothing more complicated than an off-balance vocabulary and some iffy syntax. It's English, but not as we know it.

Sometimes you can tell what was meant: "Our wine list leaves you nothing to hope for." Sometimes you can't: "Nobody is allowed to sit on the both sides of the boat." Sometimes you're not sure whether you can tell or not: the Indian hotel, for instance, that warns "No spiting on the walls." Is that "spitting" or "writing"? If the former, why only on the walls? A hotel in Beijing tells guests they have "No permission to wench." Is this a deliberately invented verb, a discreet euphemism for the professional activities of a certain kind of lady? Or do they mean something else? If so, what? "Wrench"? But what could you wrench in a hotel room? The mind boggles.

Other entries belong firmly in the "How did that happen?" file. The fake Liverpool Football Club shirts in China, for example, which have meticulously copied every last detail, right down to the club crest . . . and then turned "You'll Never Walk Alone" into "You'll Never Pickle Again." Occasionally you're left in doubt as to whether the language is wrong or not. A notice in one Shanghai hotel reads: "It is forbidden to play the recorder in guest rooms." Do they really mean "recorder"? If so, why? Has there been an epidemic of people playing that instrument? Do the Chinese take particular offense to it, even more than we do? Is that possible?

The beauty of getting lost in translation is that you never know where you'll end up. Some examples mess with your head: "If you wish, you may open the window. Do not open the Window." Some are inadvertently beautiful: "Little grass is smiling slightly, please walk on the pavement." Some verge on philosophy: "Danger comes soonest when it's despised." But whatever the effect, a chuckle is never far away.

A final word of caution. Amused as we are by other nations' fumblings with our language, we should never forget that their English is infinitely better than our Thai/Polish/Vietnamese. Indeed, sometimes it's better than our English—you'll find several examples in these pages from English-speaking nations, whether from the land of Shakespeare or the Land of the Free.

So enjoy. Go forth, take the plunge . . . and see some thoroughly *Screwed Up English*.

PLANE SPEAKING

→ You're heading for a world where the English language has been tweaked a little. The first signs come before you've even landed . . .

Dear Passenger, Wish you have a joyful journey!

When you are in public talking and laughing and drinking and singing living a happy life, suddenly you feel some part of your body is too itchy to endure.

How embarrassed! Please dial fax 01-491-02538, you will gain an unexpected result.

---➤ Chinese in-flight MAGAZINE:

We'd like to offer our affection as a gift by the white bird on sky to every genuinely go the same may together with you. This is our only requite to you.

Besides, try to prepare all you need before pack, and then, you can arrange everything's position entirely, or you will make yourself confusion.

Instructions on a KOREAN flight:

Upon arrival at Kimpo and Kimahie Airport, please wear your clothes.

Aeroflot (A SOVIET AIRLINE) advertisement:

Introducing wide boiled aircraft for your comfort.

Caption in a Chinese in-flight magazine, underneath a picture of a KILT-WEARING bagpipe player:

A man dressed in a Scottish woolen skirt blowing air whistle.

On packages of MOIST PAPER TOWELS handed out on a Chinese airline:

Healthy Wet Towel Paper

JOB RECRUITMENT advertisement for Nok Air airline, Thailand:

If you are energetic, living, friendly . . .

Chapter title from a book about the HISTORY OF THE GARUDA airline, Indonesia:

Total Quality Qontrol

On an AIRSICKNESS bag on a Spanish airplane:

Bags to be use in case of sickness or to gather remains.

We take your bags and send them in all directions.

THINGS DON'T LOOK THAT MUCH BETTER ON THE GROUND . . .

Notice on a broken turnstile at SALZBURG, AUSTRIA, passport control:

Out of work

Sign at a Beijing airport CAFÉ:

Welcome greet Presence.

At an SECURITY check at an airport in China:

Please check in animals and alcoholics. Passenger may carry 2 bottle of wine and the volume of either 1 or 2 should not be more than 1 kilogram.

Restaurant in BEN GURION Airport, Israel:

Payment Before Ordering

On a LUGGAGE TROLLEY at Singapore airport:

Not to be removed from Crewe Station.

Please stand on your turn.

For the safety of the passenger it is prohibited to carry the dangerous things in the hand bags of passenger:

1.   The hand bag
2.   The explosive materials and military
3.   Dangerous things as Gases and passions

Sign on a metal-detector scanner in France:

People with peace-maker do not pass.

At Heathrow AIRPORT, London:

No electric people carrying vehicles past this point.

CHINESE airport signs:

Soft waiting lounge

Rigidity waiting lounge

ROOM FOR IMPROVEMENT

→ You've negotiated the flight, you've battled your way through the airport—now you head for the single most prolific source of sketchy English known to mankind: the hotel. The fun starts before you even get to your room . . .

Please do not use the elevator
when it is not working.

In a HOTEL LOBBY, Beijing, China:

Good appearance please no watermelon please.

St. Petersburg, RUSSIA:

Dear Guests: Please mind your personal thinks!

←---

PARIS, France:

Please leave your values at the front desk.

-------------------------------→ PINGYAO, China:

Gussethouse

BISHKEK, Kyrgyzstan:

No entries in upper clothes.

Seoul, SOUTH KOREA:

Third floor: Turkey Bath

Peru:

Filthered weather
and ice

Zurich, SWITZERLAND:

We have nice bath and are
very good in bed.

NAME of a hotel in Lectoure, France:

Hotel de Bastard

Thailand:

Please no party in Buri Guest house and
please guiet too

You have a friend to stay with you last night (or every
night) You must pay to a money.

CZECH Republic:

Take one of our horse-driven city tours.

We guarantee no miscarriages.

Thailand (offering DONKEY rides):

Would you like to ride on your own ass?

Letter to GUESTS in a hotel in Ningbo, China:

Dear guests,

The Main Building will have some noise and nasty smell due to the interior decoration.

BAGHDAD, Iraq:

No consummation whatever may take place in this foyer.

Africa:

You may choose between a room with a view on the sea or the backside of the country.

Hamburg, Germany:

The closed window gives our climatronic the best effort.

AMALFI, Italy:

Suggestive views from every window.

BUCHAREST, Romania:

The elevator is being fixed for the next day. During that time we regret that you will be unbearable.

LEH, India:

The Old Ladakh Guest House (hospitalizing since 1974)

Seoul:

Choose twin bed or marriage size; we regret no King Kong size.

Slip and fall down carefully!

Japan:

City Hotel & Nut Club

Africa:

Mt. Kilimanjaro, the breathtaking backdrop for the Serena Lodge. Swim in the lovely pool while you drink it all in.

India:

Welcome to Hotel Cosy: where no one's stranger.

In a hotel CLOAKROOM, Berlin, Germany:

Please hang yourself here.

Cambodian HOTEL chain:

Aggressive Hotels

In the LOBBY of a Moscow hotel across from a Russian Orthodox monastery:

You are welcome to visit the cemetery where famous Russian and Soviet composers, artists, and writers are buried daily except Thursdays.

In a Tokyo hotel LAUNDRY room:

To everyone of the use, Laundromat—

Many people use a Laundromat. Let's comply with the next item to use it for the cleanness safety.

1. Let's read the explanation of the way of using it well, and use the washing machine, the dryness machine properly.

2. Let's wash a hand well before and after a wash.

3. Don't wash the person who get's an epidemic, and clothes which contacted with the person.

4. Don't wash a diaper which urine stuck to, sports shoes, an animal's rug because an unpleasantness is given to the person handled later and it is un-sanitation.

5. Let's bring it back after you spread the wash from the dryness machine and a state is done.

6. Please ask a satellite control person in charge for the inquiry about the establishment, the contact of in case of emergency.

No automobiles, Pederosts only.

Flying water in all rooms.

You may bask in sun on patio.

If service is required, give two strokes to the maid and three to the waiter.

It is kindly requested from our guests that they avoid dirting and doing rumours in the rooms.

Hot and cold water running up and down the stairs.

Left your values? And indeed your watermelon?

Good. You may now proceed to your room—where yet more delights await . . .

To call room service, please to open door and call Room Service. Please call quiet, people may sleep.

On a hotel TELEVISION set, Belgrade, Serbia:

If set breaks, inform manager.

Do not interfere with yourself.

Indonesia:

Someday laundry service.

Torremolinos, SPAIN: ◄---

Take Discotheque with or without date,
in summer plus open air bonging bar.

Cairo, EGYPT:

On September 30, winter timing will start.

As of 12:00 midnight all clocks will be forward one hour back.

---------------------------► **TOKYO, Japan:**

Is forbitten to steal hotel towels please.

If you are not person to do such thing is please not to read notis.

SHANGHAI, China:

It is forbidden to play the recorder in guest rooms.

ADVERTISEMENT for hotel in Bangkok, Thailand, includes among its amenities:

Worm Water

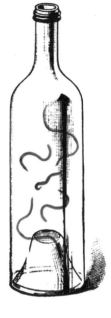

Las Palmas, CANARY Islands:

If you telephone for room service you will get the answer you deserve.

Milan, ITALY:

Our barmen will be pleased to suggest you the menu selection in the intimate atmosphere of the bar Caffe Doria or in the quiteness of your room.

Notice by a phone, Amsterdam, the NETHERLANDS:

Telephone instructions can be found on the backside.

Unfortunately the Hotel is not
endowed with restaurant.

In a Tokyo hotel BATHROOM:

Volume on. Squelch. Please dial to shut
whenever you want to.

---➤   ROME, Italy:

Please dial 7 to retrieve your auto from the garbage.

Budapest, HUNGARY:

All rooms not denounced by twelve o'clock will be paid
for twicely.

Hamburg, GERMANY:

It is our intention to pleasure you every day.

Tokyo:

Guests are requested not to smoke or do other
disgusting behaviours in bed.

If there is anything we can do to assist and help you, please do not contact us.

Vietnam:

Visitor should be not carried: arm, pets of material should be fired into the hotel.

Visitor should be not ironed-cooked-washed.

Hotel has got every service for a visitor.

GUANGDONG, **China:**

We serve you with hostiality.

Seoul, SOUTH Korea:

Measles not included in room charge.

Weifang, China:

Invisible service is available for your rest being not disturbed.

Seeduwa, Sri LANKA: ◄---

Harold Tribune is available at lobby paper rack.

Brunei:

Please keep shutters close or
monkey make you crazy.

Seoul, SOUTH Korea:

If you wish, you may open the window.

Do not open the Window.

Sriracha, THAILAND:

No in the room.

Thailand:

At the cashier's counter kindly note that personal
cheese are not accepted.

Serbia: ◄---

Voltage is 220 V but the use of the electric i rous or telt
les is not permitted.

For schedube and programmes of theaters as well as the tickets for all the types of performances, please, consult (he hall parter).

Dalat, VIETNAM:

LAUNDRY BAG

19:	Skirt	25:	Shoes
20:	Stocking	26:	Tie
21:	Hand Kerchief	27:	Price of ironing
22:	Big Towel	28:	Car with 12 to 14 seats
23:	Small Towel	29:	Car with 4 seats
24:	Hat		

Bangkok, THAILAND:

Please maintain temperature at 1 degree from 25, any higher or lower will only make the room hotter or colder.

Italy: ◄---

This hotel is renowned for its peace and solitude. In fact, crowds from all over the world flock here to enjoy its solitude.

Bosnia:

Guests should announce the abandonment of their rooms before 12 o'clock, emptying the room at the latest until 14 o'clock, for the use of the room before 5 at the arrival or after the 16 o'clock at the departure, will be billed as one night more.

SORRENTO, Italy:

The concierge immediately for informations.

Please don't wait last minutes.

Then it will be too late to arrange any inconveniences.

Welcome in your home.

We are pleased to share with you our way of living. Please listen to these few words.

The genuine antics in your room come from our family castle. Long life to it.

Please avoid coca watering, cream cleaning, wet towels wrapping and ironing drying.

For your linen we have at your disposal garden and ironing facilities.

Due to our location in the countryside, care not to throw anything (no rubber) in the toilet (WC).

Don't hesitate to use the terrace or the lounge.

More comfortable than a bar in your bed.

Have a nice stay. We'll do our best to please you and help you discovering French typical surroundings.

Leipzig, GERMANY:

Ladies, please rinse out your teapots standing upside down in sink. In no event should hot bottoms be placed on counter.

ANKARA, Turkey:

Please hang your order before retiring on your doorknob.

India:

No spiting on the walls.

Tel Aviv, ISRAEL:

If you wish breakfast, lift the telephone and our waitress
will arrive. This will be enough to bring up your food.

MADRID, Spain:

If you wish disinfection enacted in your presence, cry
out for the chambermaid.

COLOMBO, Sri Lanka:

Please do not bathe
outside the bathtub.

Switzerland:

It is defended to promenade the corridors in the boots of the mountain in front of six hours.

--→

Italy:

Please report all leakings on the part of the staff.

Hue, VIETNAM:

Toilet was cleaned and spayed.

Austria:

Not to perambulate the corridors in the hours of repose in the boots of ascension.

may I offer you a glass of water?

Copenhagen, Denmark:

Take care of burglars.

Moscow, Russia:

If this is your first visit to the USSR, you are welcome to it.

ATHENS, Greece:

Visitors are expected to complain at the office between the hours of 9 and 11 a.m. daily.

Japan:

Cooles and Heates:

If you want just condition of warm in your room, please control yourself.

Acapulco, Mexico:

The manager has personally passed all the water served here.

Hotel RATE card in Chiang Mai, Thailand:

Extra Bad—150 baht ◄----

Brasov, Romania:

Dear Guts

--- → **Serbia:**

The flattening of underwear with pleasure is the job of the chambermaid. Turn to her straightaway.

MEXICO City:

We sorry to advise you that by a electric disperfect in the generator master of the elevator we have the necessity that don't give service at our distinguishable guests.

Moscow:

The passenger must get free the room before two o'clocks of the day they are abandoning in other case, as the passenger fracture the day and must the administration pay for full.

Zurich:

Do you wish to change in Zurich?

Do so at the hotel bank!

Italy: ←--

Do not adjust yor light hanger.

If you wish more light see manager.

Japan:

Depositing the room key into another person is prohibited.

LOBBY shop in Kuantan, Malaysia:

Found in the lobby.

Japan:

Please to bathe inside the tub.

Taiwan:

Do not wear slippers to prevent falling in bath.

Thailand: ◄---

Please do not bring solicitors into your room.

Gaspe PENINSULA, Canada:

No dancing in the bathrooms!

Tokyo:

Keep your hands away from unnecessary buttons for you.

Rio de Janeiro, BRAZIL:

Visit the hairdresser in the Sub Soil of this Hotel.

France:

Wondering what to wear? A sports jacket may be worn to dinner, but no trousers.

Japan:

You are invited to take advantage of the chambermaid.

Hotel on the IONIAN Sea:

In order to prevent shoes from mislaying, please don't corridor them. The management cannot be held.

PALMA de Mallorca, Majorca:

Every Sunday very greay kocks fights at Ca'n Veta jurt in front of the ancient rase horces.

Poland:

Sweat dreams.

1.What did you look for?

2. What did you find it?

Possible "How was the service?" answers:

A. Excellent

B. The awaited one

C. Almost the awaiting one

D. Nothing

Zurich:

Because of the impropriety of entertaining guests of the opposite sex in the bedroom, it is suggested that the lobby be used for this purpose.

Beijing: ◄---

No permission to wench.

YOU'D THINK THAT IF THERE WAS ONE THING ON WHICH HOTELS WOULD MAKE THEMSELVES CLEAR, IT'D BE THEIR FIRE PROCEDURE. THINK AGAIN . . .

If you cannot reach a fire exit, close the door and expose yourself at the window.

FLORENCE, Italy:

Fire! It is what we can be doing, we hope.

No fear. Not ourselves. Say quickly to all people coming up down, everywhere, a prayer always is a clerk. He is assured of safety by expert men who are in the bar for telephone for the fighters of the fire come out.

Milan:

In case of a fire in your room and your inability to put the fire out:

Leave the room closing the door, find the exit following the signals.

Don't bother with your luggage.

Don't use the elevators (lifts).

Don't shout or run. Try to inform the desk, any personnel you might get across.

France:

In the event of fire the visitor, avoiding panic, is to walk down the corridor to warn the chambermaid.

-->

Moscow:

By all means report the fire to the floor-attendant or to any other authority of the hotel.

Copenhagen:

In the event of fire, open a window and announce your presence in a seemly manner.

Beijing:

No smoking in bed.

If it's on fire the guests should be disperse according to the safety way.

Vienna, AUSTRIA:

In case of fire, do your utmost to alarm the hotel porter.

Saudi Arabia:

<--

In case of fire, please read this.

Japan:

In case of fire, try to use the fire ex-ting wisher.

China:

Potential danger is worse than naked fire.

Precaution before salvation.

Fire can be devastating.

London: ◄ -

All fire extinguishers must be examined at least five days before any fire.

Laon, France, ENGLISH TRANSLATION of a sign in French, reading "En cas de feu—restez calme":

In case of fire do not lose your temper.

Sometimes it's even more serious than fire . . .

Tokyo:

In case of earthquake, use the torch to pass yourself out.

Feeling peckish? Why not pop down to your friendly hotel restaurant? . . .

Madrid:

Our wine list leaves you nothing to hope for.

- ➤   **Belgrade:**

Restauroom open daily.

TORREMOLINOS, Spain:

We highly recommend the hotel tart.

Ho Chi Minh City, VIETNAM:

Tasty tacos and beautiful tarts are the order of the day.

JAKARTA, Indonesia:

Wondering where to eat?

Grill and roast your clients!

Open for lunch, dinner
and Sunday brunch.

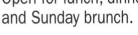

Customers who find our waitresses rude
ought to see the manager.

Bulgaria:

If you are satisfactory, tell your friends.

If you are unsatisfactory, warn the waitress.

Poland:

As for the tripe served you at the Hotel Monopol, you
will be singing its praises to your grandchildren on your
deathbed.

A La Crate Menu

Ankara:

You are invite to visit our restaurant where you can eat
the Middle East Foods in a European ambulance.

Vietnam:

Compulsory Buffet Breakfast

Miyanoshita, JAPAN:

We now have a Sukiyaki Restaurant with lodging facilities for those who want to have experiences on Japanese bedding.

Jakarta:

JP Bistro—a contemporary brassiere-style restaurant . . .

Of course, competition in the hotel industry is fierce. Owners will do anything to get your business.

Anything, that is, except check what they've written . . .

Sicilian TRAVEL brochure: ◄----

Bath in room, pavements in cooked.

REPLIES from German hotels in response to enquiries about accommodation:

We have ample garage accommodation for your char.

In the close village you can buy jolly memorials for when you pass away.

I send you my prices. If I am dear to you and your mistress she might perhaps be reduced.

We are also noted for having children.

I am honourable to accept your impossible request. Unhappy it is I here have not bedroom with bath.

A bathroom with bed I have. I can though give you a washing with pleasure in a most clean spring with no person to see. I insist that you will like this.

I am amazing diverted by your entreaty for a room.

I can offer you a commodious chamber with a balcony imminent to the romantic gorge and I hope you will want to drop in.

A vivacious stream washes my doorsteps so do not concern yourself that I am not too good in bath.

I am superb in bed.

Sorrowfully I cannot abide your auto.

Having freshly taken over the proprietry of this notorious house, I am wishful that you remove to me your esteemed costume.

Standing among savage scenery the hotel offers stupendous revelations. There is a French widow in every bedroom, affording delightful prospects.

I give personal look to the interior wants of each guest. Here you shall be well fed up, and agreeably drunk.

Our charges for weekly visitors are scarcely creditable.

Peculiar arrangements for gross parties.

Our motto is 'ever serve you right'.

A hotel should be a home from home. But then again, it's at home where most deaths occur.

Assistant public relations manager of a Jakarta hotel after a DEATH there (reported in the Jakarta Post):

Please tell the public not to kill themselves on hotel property if they want to die. It only confounds us. They can do it in the river for example.

ADVERTISEMENT for a Tokyo hotel:

Our staffs are always here waiting for you to patronize them.

Hotel BROCHURE in Qingdao, China:

Hua Tian Hotel is among the few best foreign affairs hotels.

HOTEL in Sorrento: ◀--------------------------------------

Syrene Bellevue Hotel joins a modern functional
equipment with a distinguished and smart style of the
18th century. The restaurant salon with a large view
of the Gulf of Naples, a restaurant service with a big
choice, the private beach to be reached by a lift from
inside directly, complete the undiscussable peculiarities
of this unit.

DRIVEN TO DISTRACTION

➡ **One of the easiest ways to see Screwed Up English is by car . . .**

Stop. Drive sideways.

SIGN in a hire car, Tokyo, Japan:

When passenger of foot heave in sight, tootle the horn. Trumpet him melodiously at first, but if he still obstacles your passage then tootle him with vigor.

OUTSIDE a shop in Athens, Greece:

Park one hour. Later dick dock goes the money clock.

Sign IN Tokyo:

Cars will not have intercourse on this bridge.

AND another:

Try bigger and bigger but keep more and more slowly.

ROAD sign in Kuwait:

Circle A Head

Road sign on the ISLAND of Cyprus, Greece:
Caution: Road Slippery from Grapejuice

"DEAD END" road sign, Istanbul, Turkey:
No more. Please pack up now.

Sign in Beijing, China, warning of DANGEROUS road surface:
To take notice of safe, the slippery are very crafty.

INSTRUCTIONS on Japanese driving rules:

At the rise of the hand of the policeman, stop rapidly.
Do not pass him, otherwise disrespect him.

Do not explosion the exhaust pipe.

Avoid entanglement with your wheel spoke.

Go soothingly on the grease mud
as there lurks a skid demon.

Japan road SIGN:

No parking

No stoppage

From owner's MANUAL of Toyota car:

Please not to listen to cassette while the radio is talking.

ROAD signs in India:

Avoid Overspeeding.

Always Avoid Accidents.

On the Spanish island of TENERIFE:

Road Closed: High danger of earth-falling during winding or rainy days

LUXOR, Egypt: ◄---

Parking in wrong places will make you accountalbe to law apart from being a trespassing on the right of the citizen and the state.

Traffic sign, KARACHI, Pakistan:

Please avoid accidents here.

Road SIGN in Kuwait: ▲

No P

Do not use parking lot as we expect a great deal of dustle.

Instructions at a GAS station in Tuscany, Italy:

-To insert the notes aligned to the right in any verse

-To await the accreditation in the display

-To select the wanted bomb

-Out to the spy of the select bomb, to take the supplier

In case of non-expenditure: To wait some minute and to move away the recaipt to introduce it to the agent for the refund

In a JAPANESE taxi:

Safety first.

Please put on your seatbelt.

Prepare for accident.

SIGN on a car in Manila, Philippines:

Car and owner for sale.

Japanese BROCHURE:

Toyota E-com will be come a main type of car suitable for commutation in metropolis and the suburbs nearly in the future.

Sign at a CAR repair shop in Bali, Indonesia:

Cat Oven

Solvent sold in FINLAND for unfreezing car locks:
Super piss

Sign in a pay PARKING LOT in China:
The change money partment to parking

Gas STATION, Santa Fe, New Mexico:

We will sell gasoline to anyone in a glass container.

At a MOTORING event on the French Riviera:

Competitors will defile themselves on the promenade at 11 a.m., and each car will have two drivers who will relieve themselves at each other's convenience.

On a Japanese car engine:

The ARC Product is wonders assenbiled project.

They present comfortable and unknown car life with ARC power.

On the SPARE wheel cover of a Japanese 4×4:

It's an outdoor sport that has recently started to shine. Outdoor sport is the science to raise spirits.

To choose sports for fashion or your personality.

The basic idea is to enjoy yourself.

That is important.

Another:

Nissan Terrano is for the car enthusiast who wants to feel the beat of life in his own life.

Yet ANOTHER:

Whenever and everywhere, we can meet our best friend—nature. Take a grip of steering!

On the front of a Japanese LORRY:

Challenge safe driving for the 21st century.

Sticker on the WINDSCREEN of Japanese sports car:

OFFRIMITS

On the SIDE of a Japanese van:

We think that we want to contribute to society through daiamond drilling and wire sawing.

AND on another:

Brain Location Service

ADVERT for a Japanese car:

Exciting Pleasure World accessories.

Style up Performa. ◄---

NOTICE on the windscreen of a van in London's Chinatown:

Driver on derivery

A HEALTHY RESPECT FOR LANGUAGE

If you ain't got your health, you ain't got nothin'. But if you have to deal with *Screwed Up English*, you've got even less . . .

In a MATERNITY WARD in Pumwani, Kenya:
No children allowed.

In a HOSPITAL in Barcelona, Spain:

Visitors two to a bed and half an hour only.

On a Japanese MEDICINE bottle:
Adults: 1 tablet 3 times a day until passing away.

Door to a ROOM for nursing mothers in Japan:
Suckle Room

Advertisement for a HONG KONG dentist:

Teeth extracted by the latest Methodists.

Turkish BATH in Rome:
Be pleased to come lie down with our masseuse.

She will make you forget all your tired.

Are you haunted by horribles?

Do you ever run after your nose?

Does your nose choke?

Does your head or face or shoulder ever limp?

Has any part of your body suddenly grown uncontrollable?

Advisory booklet for EXPECTANT mothers,
Public Health Centre, Joetsu City, Japan:

1. Strain yourself or push at the time of contraction and two hours later a baby will come out.

2. A swell will be checked if there is, by pushing shin.

3. If your weight gains rapidly, it is a sign of swell or fatness.

4. If you pick up around your nipple come out 1 cm high, and it'll be alright.

5. You'd better begin your sexual intercourse after the delivery after the one mouth check-up with a doctor.

6. If you want to do a vowel movement don't stop.

7. After you vomit, you rinse your mouse and if you can eat, eat.

8. You can do ãfoo, fooä naturally when you open your mouth slightly.

9. Brasure can be for maternity one or nursing bra, so that your breast can't be oppressed.

10. There are many differences of ideas in family but she felt family bondage after delivery as a wife.

On CHINESE medicine bottle:

Known to cure itching, colds, stomachs, brains, and other diseases.

On ANOTHER Chinese medicine bottle:

Expiration date: 2 years

NEWSPAPER advertisement, Manila, Philippines:

It's Summer Time!

Bring your children to the Garma Specialty Clinic for Circumcision. (Children and Adult).

Painless. Bloodless. German cut.

Barrier Free Toilet

Swedish parents EXPLAINING to an American doctor that
their daughters' thighs are bruised from a clapping game:

The girls have blue pricks.

In the office of a DOCTOR in Rome, Italy:

Specialist in women and other diseases.

SRI Lanka:

Sanitary Napking Disposal Bag

Body massage is done synchronously, to prevent parts
of the body getting over activated.

And their NASAL massage:

After the treatment you will feel very clean and more
clear nostrils.

IT'S NOT JUST A CASE OF FEELING GOOD — YOU'VE GOT TO LOOK YOUR BEST TOO ...

BARBERSHOP in Tokyo, Japan:

All customers promptly executed.

Barbershop in ZANZIBAR, Tanzania:

Gentlemen's throats cut with nice sharp razors.

LABEL on shirts sold in Japan: ◄--

FamousCrap

On a Taiwanese SHAMPOO bottle:

Use repeatedly for severe damage.

German SKIN cream:

Cream Shower for pretentious skin

BEAUTY SHOP in Chuo Rinkan, Japan:

Beauty Brain's Fantastic Fannie

Make Thin! Obesity is a well known trouble.

Fat people must not take around a majestic fatness, wearing large suits, perspirating too much.

AD in China:

Anti-falling Shampoo

Diet CENTER in Poughkeepsie, New York:

Lose all your weight: $198

Foreign guests are requested not to pull cock in tub.

Beijing, CHINA:

Haircuts half price today.

Only one per customer.

JEWELER'S window, India:

We shoot earholes.

EATING YOUR WORDS

→ Food is a universal language. We all share
a need for it, an enjoyment of it, a fascination
with it. Pity we ruin everything by making such
a mess of describing it . . .

Mad pipple

Europe:
Boiled Frogfish

On a Polish MENU:

Salad a firm's own make; limpid red beet soup with cheesy dumplings in the form of a finger; roasted duck let loose; beef rashers beaten up in the country people's fashion.

CAMBODIAN menu:

Fried internal part of chicken with mushrooms and deep fried fist with vegetables

On a menu in Rome, ITALY, for "Linguine al pesto":
Little tongues in pesto sauce

China:

Cold shredded children and sea blubber in spicy sauce

VIENNA, Austria:

Fried milk, children sandwiches, roast cattle and boiled sheep

Nepal: ◄----

Complimentary glass wine or bear

Japan:

J&J large intestine pot

Billboard in DELHI:

Hamburgers, pizzas, ice cream and snakes

France:

Nut of Holy Jacques jumped, guinea fowl stinks to it and its farce with cheese-topped dish, almost cheese-dish of mould in spice on bed of spinach

Slovakia:

Hamanegs

Shanghai, CHINA:

Our Mongolean hot pot buffet guarantees you will be able to eat all you wish until you are fed up.

French RESTAURANT in Hong Kong, under "cheeses":

Roguefart

Thai restaurant in Toronto, Canada, INDICATING the spiciest dish available:

Flames to the whole boyd.

CHINESE restaurant in London:

Assorted Meat Fried Noodle

With Meat £2.70

With Named Meat £3.50

With Other Meat £4.60

CANBERRA, Australia:

Dumping soup

Thailand:

Rather burnt land slug

Curly flower

General Chaos Chicken

We are also have fun food you are never had before.

We are always look for new food.

Thank you for eating our delicious food.

We will never stop creating your tasted food.

Steamed fillet of new zeal and orange roughy

Quality kept foods warm.

Fresh thousand year old eggs

Salad: cucumber, salad sheets, mayonnaise, ovum

SPICY dish at a Chinese restaurant in Memphis, Tennessee: ◄--------------

. . . will make you cry silently.

Sexy calamari leg

Restaurant in San Juan, Puerto Rico, SERVING crab and conch:

Grab and crunch

China:

Mr Zheng and his fellow workers like to meet you and entertain you with hostility and unique cooking technique.

Chinese restaurant in Toronto, DESCRIBING boneless chicken:

Bong lens chicken

FROM Japanese menus: ◄--------------------------------------

Savour best match of the mysterious sauces.

Modernly arranged miscellaneous European Flavors.

Vietnam bird salad, mixed Chimaki and asian corses.

Seasonal ingredients specially pre-pared and directly imported from their place of origination.

Kansas City, MISSOURI:

Ho-made Chili

Indian restaurant in GRANTHAM, UK:
Brinjal bhaji (Aborigine)

CAFÉ in Smithfield Market, London:
Chinese fried noddle

Café in the EMPIRE State Building, New York:

All our eggs made with 3 omeletes.

Café IN London:
Jacket potato with
mixed vegetable cause

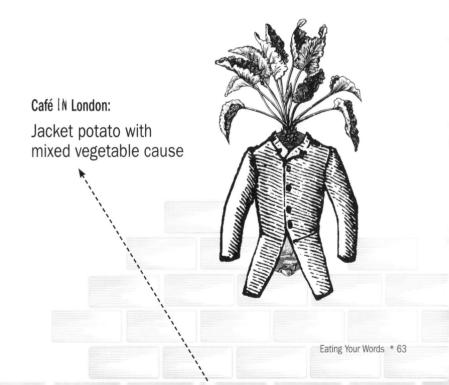

And, as one of its SANDWICH fillings:

Smocked salmon

Athens, Greece:

Chopped cow with a wire through it and bowels in sauce

Greek MENU:

Spleen omelet, fisherman's crap soup,
calf pluck, bowels

CAFÉ in London:

Jacked potatoes

And for dessert . . .

Japan:

Strawberry crap ←- -

Europe:

Sweat from the trolley

China, DESCRIBING a pancake dish:

Waiter will roll in front of you.

Costa RICA:
Pastry Chef

Thailand:

Waffies

Would you like anything to drink with that? . . .

Europe:

Garlic coffee

Japan:

Ginger Bumping Milk

INGOLSTADT, Germany:
Coffee and snakes

India:

Our establishment serves tea in a bag like mother.

Wine List

Larger

Carlsberg—Pint

That's just the food itself—service is not included . . .

Malaysia:

Seafood brought in by customers will not be entertained.

Please do not bring outside food excluding children under five.

Paris, FRANCE:

We serve five o'clock tea at all hours.

India:

After one visit we guarantee you will be regular.

Japan:

This place cannot eat and drink with the thing which you brought in.

Italy:

Please pay the house waiter the price of your consummation. ←- - - - - - - - - -

Hong KONG:

Come broil yourself at your open table.

NEON sign outside a restaurant in China:

Smart noshery makes u slobber.

Swiss MOUNTAIN inn:

Special today—no ice cream.

RESTAURANT in the Swiss Alps: ←- -

No skies inside.

they will be charged 400 baht cockage.

contemporary closed.

Michigan:

The early bird gets the worm!

Special shoppers' luncheon before 11 a.m.

Employees must wash your hands.

Chelsea, LONDON: ◄---------------------------------------

Plat du jour, changed each day.

MUMBAI, India:

Seven days a week and weekends too.

Japanese restaurant in OCEANSIDE, California:

Test our pride.

Tokyo restaurant ADVERTISEMENT:

Colorful dining space surrounded by stained glasses.

SIGN in a Chinese restaurant, U.S.:

Warning: Tips for waitress not privilege off customer, and not optonal to do! Is custimarry and is the law for leave tips, otherwise is possibul to face prostection by law! Please be responsivele, leave tip and no go jail! Have a nice day!

Sign in a London PIZZA restaurant:

Open 24 hours except 2 a.m.–8 a.m.

Thailand:

For our convenience, we do not accept checks.

On one Chinese menu, various dishes are marked with an ASTERISK. At the bottom of the page, it states . . .

the asterisk means handicapped accessible.

With deepest respect, we hope to wish our insistence you washes your hands when using our facility.

VIETNAMESE restaurant in U.S.:

Troublemakers will be Bard!

Have Nice Day.

We will be honouring your delivering in the fast time as possible.

No surrender!

Eat as much as your tummy can challenge!

Chinese restaurant in Charlotte, North CAROLINA:

No MSG. We care you health.

Chinese restaurant in BROOKLYN, New York:

Fast free delivery by the cars.

Sign on the door of an Italian restaurant, Osaka, Japan:

Hospitality now, or in 10 minutes.

We do not re-use the food.

VARIOUS Chinese restaurants in the U.S.:

We can alter the spicy according to your wishes.

We delivery ahead.

Lunch Buffet: $4.99

Chicken 3–8 years old: $2.95

Indian restaurant in LONDON:

We are established since 1963.

Our first restaurant was arranged to be open on Saturday 23rd November—the same day as the Kennedy assassination happened. [It was actually the 22nd.] It was a loss of a very important person all over the world.

When it comes to Chinese food, sometimes the name of the restaurant says it all . . .

KUALA Lumpur, Malaysia:

Soon Go Fatt

Baltimore, MARYLAND:

Eat Must Be First

PITTSBURGH, Pennsylvania:

My Dung

Princeton, New JERSEY:

Wild Oily

NIGHT-TIME IS THE RIGHT TIME

→ You're wined and dined—now
you want a night on the town.
Trouble is, the town isn't making
things all that clear . . .

CAIRO, Egypt:
Unaccompanied ladies not admitted unless with husband or similar.

Sign outside a BAR in Kyoto, Japan:

Bar, Isn't It?

SHANGHAI, China:
Restaurant and bra

Sign outside a Mexican DISCO:
Members and non-members only

ADVERTISEMENT for a disco, Luxembourg:

Let's fun.

SIGN outside a Mexican bar:
Sorry, we're open!

In a bar in Tokyo, JAPAN:
Special cocktails for the ladies with nuts.

Young men's balls in full swing.

Sign on a bar in Thailand called HIPPIES Bar & Restaurant:

Green peace recycle time

Recycle can of beer after you drink it

Save your nature happy green like.

SIGN outside a bar in Bangkok, Thailand:

The shadiest cocktail bar in town.

Norway:

Ladies are requested not to have children in the bar.

From a brochure for a supper club at AMBASSADOR City
Jomtien resort, Pattaya, Thailand:

Relieve yourself in an ideal of karaoke and live music in bewitching time.

Of course, you could always set your cultural sights a little higher . . .

A place in Seville. Procession of Ball-fighters.

The roaring of balls is heard in the arena. Aria and chorus: 'Toreador, Toreador. All hail the Balls of a toreador.' Enter Don Jose singing, 'I besmooch you.' Carmen repels him. He stabbs her.

Aria: 'Oh, rupture, rupture.'

- - - - ➤ Notice at Bolshoi THEATRE, Moscow, Russia:

We ask to excuse for the possible caused inconveniences in connection with work on reconstruction of theatre.

TESTED TO INSTRUCTION

→ The modern world is a stressful place. But don't worry, there are countless gadgets and devices on hand to make life easier. Just remember the golden rule when operating them: Never read the instructions first . . .

Hong Kong alarm CLOCK:

To set alarm set alarm hand to time desired to wake. To change time desired to wake, reset alarm to the time desired to.

Swedish flat-packed CABINET:

It is advisory to be 2 people during assembly.

Japanese HEMORRHOID treatment:

Lie down on bed and insert product slowly up to the projected portion like a sword-guard into anal duct. while inserting product for approximatly 5 minuites, keep quiet.

Telus LG1000, a Korean MOBILE phone aimed at ages eight to twelve:

Open-minded: Easy-to-use in Structure.

Getting along with you, I reveal my secret to you, buddy.

Despite such strengths listed above, I need enough food to get energy.

For you to see me, get to know me more and hang out with me longer.

My favorite food is battery!

When I am tired, please give my words to your parents to energize me.

Or I have to go to bed without seeing you.

Let's not make a scene when we meet not to disturb others especially in class or library.

INSTRUCTIONS on instant meal in China: ◄---

Eat after turning round in high microwave for three minutes. You will enjoy this quality eating experience.

Leaflet found by a HOMEOWNER (the homeowner couldn't remember—or imagine—which appliance the leaflet came with):

The washers contained into the kit must be absolutely assembled also when the manifold is without them.

This product was easy to burning, aloof the high temperature, please. Because maybe beget any danger and the product's definition distort.

The product have some keenness part, so need to prevent bruise. The product only befit measure and study, unable to do other definition's measure. Needed the pater-familias accompany, if the children haven't 3 years.

On an ELECTRIC amplifier that was supposed to be grounded: ◄--

Warning: This appliance must be earthed.

Chinese headset MAGNIFYING glass:

Maintance: This product is made of acrylic.

So don't rub by chemical medicine to avoid lens spoiled. Just use medium alcohol to rub it lightly. Watch carefully for use.

MP3 player:

Pause now you are in shortly, stop.

Taiwanese SPANNER:

Easy to use, it is only a simple Ratchet-Action.

The more tension. The more steady, while in operation.

-------------------------------------→ Chinese RED warning light:

Suitable for bi cycle, jogging, climbing, baby-car, disable-
car. Especially for the children, blind men, old men, in
the morning or evening, and the cloudy day, when the
bright is not enough, to increase more safety.

CHINESE travel clock:

Attention before you use it. 1. Please pull out the PVC
insulation sheet Beside the battery-cover on the bottom,
Then the Music will come up.

Press any Key to stop it. This is regular situation.

Chinese CANDLE: ◄-----
Keep this candle out of children.

Chinese SCOOTER:

Safe drive notice to the motorcycle drivers.

There is the condition for you to drive a motorcycle Safely and make it serve to you faithfully The condition is to keep the safety in your mind forever.

TAIWANESE room spray:

Can be used at any place where needs to eliminate the stinky smell and keep fleshing surroundings at all time.

Chinese bath SPONGE: ◄--

Pull with your hands and stick it on your body, you will feel great as bathing.

TAIWANESE puzzle toy:

Let's decompose and enjoy assembling!

Chinese model kit, stating that paint and glue are not INCLUDED:

This kit cannot be completed with paint and glue.

CHINESE toy:

Avoid disturbing the other while enjoying this item.

During cutting, do not put your head too close.

There is difference between up and down.

Beware of being swallowed by child, due
to small parts.

On a toy box for a toy CAR manufactured in China:

Let Tear Away in You Fancy DriveWayThe Fond
DriveWayYou Doing Youself

On the same BOX, close-up pictures from different angles of the toy labeled:

Foreside's Bottom

Rearward's Bottom

Install's Way

On a Chinese toy BOAT:

Please don't place it in following place:

(a) nearby strong vibration. (b) in the dusty play.

Taiwanese wading BOOTS:

Warning! Difficult to swim out if wearing wader filled with water by falling down! Therefor, please avoid deep water where danger of drowning possibility exists.

------------------------➤ **Pack of toy ANIMALS sold in Ranong, Thailand:**

Be careful of being eaten by small children.

JAPANESE phone card:

1. Lift up receiver. 2. Insert phone card. 3. Dial 0999 + number. 4. Say Hello.

Japanese RADIO:

You will know radio on by enchanting green light.

Japanese TELEPHONE: ◄---

Plug the phone jack into the wall. If the phone rings, pick it up and greet the person on the other end by saying 'Hello!' or another such greeting.

Once completing your conversation, hang up the phone.

Chinese COMPUTER monitor:

Please be sure to keep the vents on top open.

Do not bring spillables near these,
like chicken soup and dust.

PHONE in Japanese hotel:

For long distance Dial 0 and Aria Cord.

CASHPOINT screen, Taiwan:

When operating the Automatic Teller Machine (ATM), you
should keep attention on the screen.

Do not believe any indications that you can operate the
ATM with a cell phone, telephone, or leaflets.

GREEK deodorant stick:

Push up bottom.

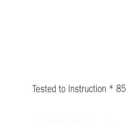

Japanese washing MACHINE:

Push button.

Foam coming plenty.

Big noise.

Finish.

In a PACK of batteries in Austria:

Do not swallow Baterries or it could make you a seriously hurt blood stream, or could make your mind damaged.

Instructions with CHINESE exercise balls:

Three types of ball are offered.

They are one. two. three.

SOMETIMES, THERE'S AN AWFUL LOT TO BE SAID FOR THE STRAIGHTFORWARD APPROACH . . .

On a fire EXTINGUISHER, Calcutta (Kolkata), India: ◄-----------------

Cease Fire.

2ND AVE

TRANSPORT TROUBLE

⟶ It's often said that travel broadens the mind. It seems to do the opposite for the vocabulary . . .

On a ferry from TENERIFE to La Gomera, Canary Islands:

Keep this ticket up the end of your trip.

Sign on underground, in SHANGHAI, China, informing passengers that the way out is up the stairs:

Exit—make-up.

In Tokyo, JAPAN:

Please get off a bicycle.

Notice in a SLEEPING carriage on Indian train:

Do not invite thieves to sleep in the floor.

On a Vietnamese BOAT:

Nobody is allowed to sit on the both sides of the boat.

On a Japanese TOURIST map:

Shitseeing Bus Stop

Bus Stop

Train STATION in Poprad, Slovakia:

Dear passengers,

The railwaypolice take the liberty of daring you not to trust for keeping guard on your personal things and baggage to unknown persons. Please, do not enable theft of your baggage through falling asleep or walking away.

Sign ONBOARD ship in Mobile, Alabama:

Warning: despite our best efforts, park exhibits slip, fall, head strike, cut, pinch, ankle twist, spray paint mist, particle breathing, alligator bite, heat lightning, and stress risks—particularly to unsupervised children, rambunctious youths and over exerted adults.

ON a Vietnamese boat:

Nobody is allowed to sit on the both sides of the boat.

Beijing, CHINA:

When leaving the bus please be careful of your victim.

In LOBBY of Tokyo Tower, Tokyo, Japan:
Don't smoke while walking.

--→ **On a Soviet SHIP in the Black Sea:**

Helpsavering apparata in emergings behold many whistles! Associate the stringing apparata about the bosoms and meet behind. Flee then to the indifferent lifesavering shippen obediencing the instructs of the vessel chef.

FERRY in San Juan, Puerto Rico, harbor:

In case of emergency, the lifeguards are under the seat in the center of the vessel.

Near the Vélo-Rail in FRANCE:

In case of no respect of the security rules, the responsability of the direction couldn't involved.

Beijing, CHINA: ←--------------------------------------

Danger prohibited aboard this boat.

Indonesian TRAVEL brochure:

If we are lucky we will see duck boys home, men massaging their cocks on the road, cow boys taking grass. Yes it is a wonderful experience.

In a travel AGENCY in Barcelona, Spain:

Go away.

Caption for a PHOTO, in a Japanese magazine, of a London Routemaster bus:

Double dicker.

SIGN at the ferry terminal in Davao, Philippines:

Adults: 1 USD

Child: 50 cents

Cadavers: subject to negotiation.

Sign at a waterfall in BRAZIL:

Dear Visitors:

The elevator Trail of de falls is closed for maintenance.
The return shoued be made by de stairs. The wai up
has about 200 meters with an inclination of 15% and
150 steps. Apologize us for detemporary inconvenience.

In this Expedition you will know the highets waterfall in the world. From Canaima, through the Sabana, the Jungles and the rivers Carrao and Churun, you'll enjoy one of the biggets emotions of this life. And the facilities Camp. Guides as natives, all experts, will bring you trough troubles waters, just where a few have made it. Be you one of them. Meals in open fire never taste so goo.

In taxis in Beijing, China, an ELECTRONIC voice reminds you:

Please do not forget anything that you take with you.

Sign near Victoria Station, LONDON:

Closed for official opening

FRENCH tourist brochure:

In France, you can cruise on many canals and see the peculiarities.

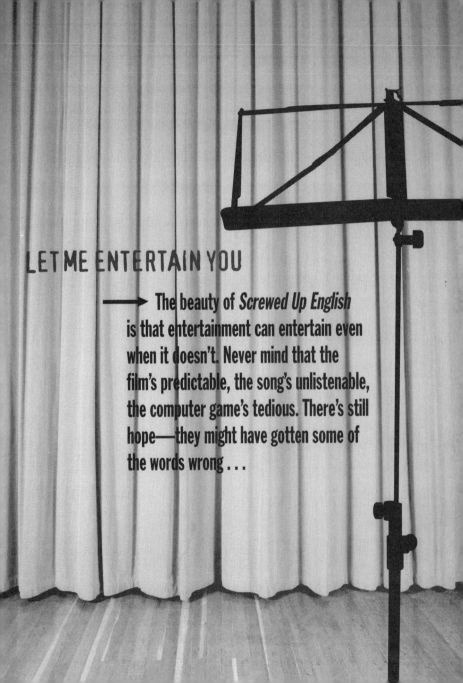

LET ME ENTERTAIN YOU

➡ The beauty of *Screwed Up English* is that entertainment can entertain even when it doesn't. Never mind that the film's predictable, the song's unlistenable, the computer game's tedious. There's still hope—they might have gotten some of the words wrong . . .

VIDEOS available in Hong Kong:

Fargo: *Mysterious Murder in Snowy Cream*

The Full Monty: *Six Stripped Warriors*

The English Patient: *Don't Ask Me Who I Am*

Boogie Nights: *His Powerful Device Makes Him Famous*

Nixon: *The Big Liar*

The Professional: *This Hit Man Is Not As Cold As He Thought*

Good Will Hunting: *Bright Sun, Just Like Me*

Dead Poets Society: *Bright Sun In Heavy Rain*

As Good As It Gets: *Mr. Cat Poop*

Pirated videos in SURINAME:

Deep Throat: *Deep Trout*

Death on the Nile: *Dead on the Nail*

- - - - - - - - - - - - - - - - ➤
Advertisements for FILMS being shown in Taiwan:

Six Days, Seven Nights: After *Air Force One*, Harrison Ford is flying a airplane, again!

Small Soldiers: The style of characters is phat, special effects are cool, this film is phat and cool.

The Avengers: The perfect style with a great taste to save the world.

English subtitles from films AVAILABLE in Hong Kong:

Same old rules: no eyes, no groin.

I have been scared shitless too much lately.

This will be of fine service for you, you bag of the scum. I am sure you will not mind that I remove your manhoods and leave them out on the dessert floor for your aunts to eat. Yah-hah, evil spider woman! I have captured you by the short rabbits and can now deliver you violently to your gynecologist for a thorough extermination.

Greetings, large black person. Let us not forget to form a team up together and go into the country to inflict the pain of our karate feets on some ass of the giant lizard person.

The Iceman COMETH:

I threat you! I challenge you meet me on the roof tonight for a duet!

I will kill you until you are dead from it!

He started it first!

The Kung Fu Cult MASTER:

Just scold Chang as 'Shame-less asshole' for three times.

Then you will free from this kind of suffer forever.

You will not happy ending!

The Kung Fu Cult MASTER:

Master, where are those people of Ming Sect? They seem to be disappeared.

ONCE UPON A TIME in China and America:

I've to cut partial of my freedom.

Dr Wai and the Scripture Without WORDS: ◄-------------------------------

He is jealousing!

It is destinated to be you!

Lethal PANTHER:

The bullets inside are very hot.

Why do I feel so cold?

As Tears GO By:

I got knife-scars more than the number of your leg's hair!

Holy WEAPON:

I am damn unsatisfied to be killed in this way.

PEDICAB Driver:

Fatty, you with your thick face have hurt my instep.

POM POM and Hot Hot: ◄-------------

I'll fire aimlessly if you don't come out!

You are too useless. And now I must beat you.

Rich and FAMOUS:
Gun wounds again?

BRAIN Theft:
A normal person wouldn't steal pituitaries.

Pedicab DRIVER:
You always use violence.

I should've ordered glutinous rice chicken.

The SEVENTH Curse:
Take my advice, or I'll spank you without pants.

SAVIOUR of the Soul:
Beware! Your bones are going to be disconnected.

Police STORY 2:
Beat him out of recognizable shape!

Armour of GOD:
Who gave you the nerve to get killed here?

THE Beheaded 100:

How can you use my intestines as a gift?

--->

On the RUN:

Quiet or I'll blow your throat up.

SATYR Monks:

You daring lousy guy.

Pedicab DRIVER:

Damn, I'll burn you into a BBQ chicken!

Tag line on a Chinese DVD copy of The Matrix REVOLUTIONS: ◄----------------

The White Men

Wanted A Stud To Breed Slaves.

It's not just movies where things go wrong . . .

Quotes from Western films SHOWN in Japan:

Forrest Gump, for "My momma always said life was like a box of chocolates. You never know what you're gonna get': "The life where Mama was said always seemed like the box of the chocolate. The profit which does not know those which are gonna under any condition do."

Dirty Harry, for "You've got to ask yourself a question: 'Do I feel lucky?' Well, do ya, punk?": "It asks 1 in you yourself, it becomes: 'As for me fortunately is felt?' To be good, as for ya and punk?"

Casablanca, for "Of all the gin joints in all the towns in all the world, she walks into mine": "In all towns of the all worlds of all gin, her it connects to my ones which you walk."

JAPANESE copy of a Meatloaf album includes the tracks:

"You Took The Words Right Out Of My Mouse"
and (for "Two Out Of Three Ain't Bad")
"Sixty Six Per Cent Is All Right"

Bootleg CD available in China:

Seargent Peeper's Lonely Hearts Club Band

AND, by the same band:
"Hey Tube"

On an Indonesian BOOTLEG U2 album:

"Angle of Harlem"

CAPTION in a Japanese magazine next to picture of famous actor:
Jude Low

AND THAT'S OFFICIAL

→ They can lock you up, take your money and ask you lots of impertinent questions. So it's nice to know that when it comes to language, the powers that be sometimes have powers that aren't . . .

VIETNAMESE customs form:

Objects must be declared.

If there isn't any object mark X only at the quantity Yes column and if there are any objects, cross out letter No and at the same row write exact amount of weight of these objects in words or in figures.

Same FORM forbids:

Giving false declaration or having the action of tricking.

On a Chinese tourist BUREAU sign:

Service for the Unit

Letter sent by Rotterdam POLICE:

You did not report yourself by the Alien police.

You have to do this in a short time, otherwise you get troubles! When you don't come to our office, we demand you to come!

And when you don't come again, you maybe have to pay a fine, and it is possible that you will be expanded.

On a Hungarian VISA form:

Your answers should be typewritten or printed in case of handwriting.

RECORDED information line, Australia (set up to answer questions about the new Goods and Services tax plan):

If you understand English, press 1.

If you do not understand English, press 2.

From a MEETING in the European Commission:

The chairman called the meeting to order and asked if there were any matters to discuss under the table.

SHOP SOILED

→ **The first rule of retail is that the customer is always right. The second seems to be that the grammar is always wrong . . .**

JALAPENO
99¢
LB

In a Majorcan SHOP:

English well talking here speeching American.

In an Israeli BUTCHER'S:

I slaughter myself twice daily.

Shop in BUDAPEST, Hungary:

Very smart! Almost pansy!

A STORE in Barcelona, Spain is just named: ◄---

Broke

Shop sign on Lovina Beach in Bali, INDONESIA:

Feel like shopping? We have no good things to sell.

DOOR of ice cream shop in Iran:

Baskin-Robbins—Where Never Wonder Cease

On a liquor store in GREECE:

So remember if you find a better price elsewhere, don't buy it because we have the best.

NOTICE in a dry cleaner's window in Bangkok, Thailand:

Drop your trousers here for the best results.

Grocer's shop, JAPAN:
Flesh Food

Sign OUTSIDE Chinese store:

We try our best to decrease your life.

On a pizza TAKE-OUT and delivery place in Prague, Czech Republic:
Pizza Go Home

Name of SHOP in Medan, Indonesia:

68% Perfect Shop

CLOTHES shop in Paris, France:
Dresses for street walking.

Sign next to small STATUES for sale, Kamakura, Japan:

Japanese Happy Thing, All 500 Yen

LAUNDRY in Rome, Italy:

Ladies, leave your clothes here and spend the afternoon having a good time.

Sign over a PET store in Osaka, Japan:

Fondle dogs.

Store in Amman, JORDAN:

Visit our bargain basement—one flight up.

In the same STORE they sell:

Pork Handbags

ON a reusable bag in Kyoto, Japan:

It is great and I want you who are the bag which is easy to use to surely use.

Swedish furrier:

Fur coats made for ladies from their own skin.

Outside a TAILOR'S in Hong Kong:

Ladies may have a fit upstairs.

SHOP in Tokyo, Japan:

Our nylons cost more than common, but you'll find they are best in the long run.

On a Japanese SHOPPING bag:

Now baby.

Tonight I am feeling cool and hard boiled.

On ANOTHER:

Switzerland: seaside city.

ADVERTISEMENT for a Tokyo antique shop:

This shop has been moved to the present place for 35 years.

Brand name in JAPAN on a tote bag:

Casual Style Hump

TAILOR in Rhodes, Greece:

Order your summers suit. Because is big rush, we will execute customers in strict rotation.

Sign in a SHOP on the island of Cozumel, Mexico:

Broken English Spoken Perfectly

Notice on a soup terrine in a German cash-and-carry store:

Pie Soup

In Japanese record store, records are CLASSIFIED in these categories, among others:

Hard Rock, Gram Rock

Chiseled in the marble façade of a Japanese CLOTHING shop:

Dresses for ladies and gentlemen.

This merchandise is to be used for turning a trick on Halloween.

---------→ On a FABRIC label on material in a Wal-Mart in Ontario, Canada:
100% unknown

TURKISH shop:
All peoples welcome for the gifts.

Clothes shop in BRUSSELS, Belgium: ◄---
Mourning and sportswear

GIFT shop in Nice, France:
Our police: no return, no exchange

For your convenience, we recommend coitus, efficient self-service.

Shop in SHANGHAI, China, aiming for "Cashier":
Accept Silver.

In the WINDOW of a Japanese store:

We wish you are Merry Christmas.

Philippines photographic firm SPECIALIZING in bridal photos:

You tie the knot, we freeze you.

Vietnam:

Opening time: From 8H30 to 17H00

Day in, day out

STORE in Tokyo:

Welcome to the best place where makes you happy.

Advertisement for a wedding shop in the Enfield Independent (London):

Bridesmaids from £65

Price is a very important factor in any purchase . . .

Hong Kong store, advertising a final CLEARANCE:

Anal Clearance

Cards HANDED out in front of shop, Mexico:

Come to Juan's Jewelry Shop.

We won't screw you too much.

SHOP in Sapporo, Japan, announcing a sale:

Beat the price off!

In the window of an INDIAN shop:

Why go somewhere else to be cheated when you can come here?

ALL PART OF THE PACKAGE

→ **Never judge a book by its cover, they say. But should you judge a product by its packaging?**

On a JAPANESE food processor:

Not to be used for the other use.

On a Japanese TOOTHPASTE:

Gives you strong mouth and refreshing wind!

On back of an MP3 player MADE in China: ◄- -

Testes to Comly

With FCC Standards

WARNING label on a Chinese lint-cleaning roller:

1. Do not use this roller to the floorings that made of wood and plastic.

2. Do not use this roller to clean the stuffs that dangerous to your hands such as glass and chinaware.

3. Do not use the roller to people's head, it is dangerous that hair could be sticked up to cause unexpected suffering.

On the back of a NIGHTLIGHT made in China:

This night lamp series is elegant in appearance.

It adopts advanced electric circuit and material.

It is safe and energy-saving.

There are several colors of light for choice.

The white color is high brightness suitable for using at the corridor, staircase and bathroom.

The yellow, pink and light blue coldes are suitable for bedroom their gentle light will not dazzle while sleeping.

The green color is suitable for karaoke room and decoration cabinet.

It brings comfort and romantic feeling to your home

JAPANESE soft drinks:

Wo! Monkey Fizz

Wo! Salty Cat

Clean Finger Nail—Chinese tissues

Kolic—Japanese mineral water

Creap Creamy Powder—Japanese Coffee Creamer

Last Climax—Japanese tissues

Ass Glue—Chinese glue

Swine—Chinese chocolates

Libido—Chinese soda

Ban Cock—Indian cockroach repellent

Shocking—Japanese chewing gum

Homo sausage—East Asian fish sausage

Cat Wetty—Japanese moistened hand towels

Hornyphon—Austrian video recorder

Chocolate Colon—Japanese cookie

Shitto—Ghanian pepper sauce

Pipi—Yugoslavian orangeade

Polio—Czechoslovakian laundry detergent

Superglans—Netherlands car wax

I'm Dripper—Japanese instant coffee

Zit—Greek soft drink

My Fanny—Japanese toilet paper

Colon Plus—Spanish detergent

On a range of PRODUCTS produced by a Japanese company:
Too fast to live, too young to happy.

Russian AMMUNITION box:

Hurting cartridges

KOREAN soft candy:
Farm Chew

The whisper amplifier device is a micro one used for someone who rare to hear or interception.

CLOCKWORK toy made in Hong Kong:

Guaranteed to work throughout its useful life.

Japanese TOY:

Danger! A dangerous toy. This toy is being made for the extreme priority the good looks.

The little part which suffocates when the sharp part which gets hurt is swallowed is contained generously.

Only the person who can take responsibility by itself is to play.

On the BOX of a Chinese-made CD cabinet:

Run From Opposite Direction Cabinet

Free More Funny!

Increase Brain.

Interesting.

Amused.

FOOD PACKAGING IS A PARTICULAR BANE OF MODERN LIFE. DAYS CAN PASS AS YOU TRY IN VAIN TO OPEN A PACKAGE OF CHEESE. AT LEAST NOW YOU'VE GOT SOMETHING TO LAUGH AT DURING THE STRUGGLE...

On a sticker on a PEAR in China:

Asian Rear

Crème brûlée in a Paris SUPERMARKET:

Preheat your oven on grill, strew your cream with sugar. Knock over the recipient to get rid of the excess. Let the cream warm for few minutes before eating.

Jar of JAM in India:

Contains no fruit whatsoever.

Instructions on a PACKET of convenience food from Italy:

Besmear a backing pan, previously buttered with a good tomato sauce, and, after, dispose the cannelloni, lightly distanced between them in a only couch.

On a package of Japanese CANDIES:

At last! A not too sticky calcium enriched soft-candy that's both healthy and tasty!

JAPANESE low-fat yogurt:

For Gourmet and Ladies

On a Japanese Coca-Cola CAN:

I feel Coke & sound special.

On a BOX of Chinese cookies:

Pure Europe taste.

Give you the authentic exotic flavor.

Veritable Material.

Nourishment Abumdance.

On a Japanese CHOCOLATE bar:

Soft and mild, like a Japanese woman.

Good flavor and full of juice.

On a Japanese TEA bag:

Do not wet with water.

CHINESE tea box:

Flower Face Tea

On a Russian ice cream BAR:

Do not taste our Ice Cream when it is too hard.

Please continue your conversation until the Ice Cream grows into a softer. By adhering this advisement you will fully appreciate the wonderful Soviet Ice Cream.

On a BAG of candy from China:

Its translucent color so alluring and taste and aroma so gentle and mellow offer admiring feelings of a graceful lady. Enjoy soft a juicy Kasugai Muscat Gummy.

On a Japanese food PACKAGE:

This cute mild curry uses 100% Japanese apple and cheerful hamster.

LABEL on the Japanese soft drink Pocari Sweat:

Highly recommended as a beverage for such activities as sports, physical labor, after a hot bath, and even as a eye-opener in the morning.

UCC Mocha Blend Coffee label, JAPAN: ◄--

This coffee has the smooth and harmonious taste with full of aroma.

UCC Drink It BLACK **Coffee label, Japan:**

Black coffee has great features which other coffees have never had: Non-sugar.

BOTTLED beverage for sale in Ontario, Canada:

Bloody Zit

On a bag of sweets BOUGHT in London:

Sweet candy, taste of pure candy, bring a pleasure.

On a BOX of ChocoBouchees, a Japanese chocolate dessert cake:

Confidence of creating deliciousness.

This tastiness can not be carried even by both hands.

Label on an orange-flavored DRINK, Japan:

This light and smooth taste drink is the best refreshment to you. Anytime, anywhere, just like your friend.

KASUGAI Fruit Gummy snacks, Japan:

The gorgeous taste of fully ripened pineapple, imposing as a southern island king crowned in glory, is yours to enjoy in every soft and juice Kasugai Pineapple Gummy.

Its translucent color so alluring and taste and aroma so gentle and mellow offer admiring feelings of a graceful lady. Enjoy soft and juicy Kasugai Muscat Gummy.

FROM a Tokyo trade guide:

Daily sweat is nullified by this admirable coffee set at free chatting. You can afford to grind coffee grains while having coffee itself & enjoying hand works to powder, befitted to lay on the interior item made of wooden at anywhere wanted to.

Coffee fragrance matches to the article in a cute and quiet circumstance.

In an Italian advertising CAMPAIGN:

Schweppes Toilet Water

In JAPAN:

Rice Scoop—A fashionable kitchen tool, makes your life colorful and pleasant.

FRENCH cheese:

This crud is from the finest milk solely from the cows of the Brie region.

SIGN LANGUAGE

→ There's something particularly beautiful about a sign that doesn't say what it really means. All that effort, all that metal, all that paint—but no one stopped to check the words . . .

Sign on the GRASS in a Paris park:

Please do not be a dog.

TEMPLE in Burma:

Footwearing strictly prohibited.

In NAPLES, Italy:

Dear Customer:

Please control your change before leaving the ticket desk.

Indian national PARK:

Notice:

Ramganga River is inhabited by crocodiles.

Swimming is prohibited.

Survivors will be prosecuted.

SIGN in China:

Meet Carefully

Tibet:

Reception Centre for the Unorganised Tourists

STREET sign in Japan:

Waiting Will Be Prosecuted.

In SOUTH Korean train station:

For Restrooms, go back toward your behind.

Sign in LE TOUQUET, France:

Instructions to Users of the ascenseur, Persons ignorant of the maneuvers of the ascenseur are prayed instantly to address themselves to the concierge.

Sign POSTED in Germany's Black Forest:

It is strictly forbidden on our Black Forest camping site that people of different sex, for instance, men and women, live together in one tent unless they are married with each other for that purpose.

In Cuba a "slippery floor" sign READS:

The floor slides.

On a tap in a FINNISH washroom:

To stop the drip, turn cock to right.

Renovating with curtsy to history: The elevator in the East pier is currently being widely upgraded. The current renovation involves updating these controls to the latest state of the art. Société Nouvelle d'exploitation de la Tour Eiffel apologises for all the temporary inconveniences.

Chinese SIGN:

Little grass is smiling slightly, please walk on the pavement.

Sign in RESIDENTIAL area in British Columbia, Canada:

Caution: Live Children Playing

AMUSEMENT ride, Saudi Arabia:

For your safety this game is not allowed for those who suffer from hearts, diabetics, nerves, high pressure and pregnants.

- ► Next to staircase in KYOTO, Japan:

This area is entranse second floor. Don't shit down!!

BANK in Bucharest, Romania:

Count change over the counter.

Ulterior complaints are not listened.

Next to a POND in China:

Take care! Fall into water carefully!

In a bathroom in Thailand:

Please do not flash toilet paper in the toilet!

The GOVERNMENT in Seoul, South Korea, established a hotline for taxi passengers who encountered rudeness. A sign in taxis advised of this:

Intercourse Discomfort Report Center

It is forbidden to enter a woman even a foreigner if dressed as a man.

ISLAND of Zakynthos, Greece:

Attention: It is forbitten to curry wet things.

A private school in NAIROBI, Kenya:

No trespassing without permission.

OKLAHOMA CITY, Oklahoma:

No dumping—trespassers will be violated.

Calcutta (KOLKATA), India:

Do not spit here and there.

AND another:

Commit no nuisance.

On the side of a TRASH can apparently intended for
fruit skins or seed and nut shells in China:

Fruit leather suitcase

Sign in a park in CHINA:

Cherishing every tree and piece of grass, they give you
relaxed and happy.

AND another one in the same park:

Monkey is the important member in biosphere, to
protect it is to protect human being itself.

Japanese "Do not enter" SIGN:

Don't get into this.

On the DOOR of a gelato shop in Venice, Italy:

The cone and the plastic-cup are only to export. Thank
you.

Malaysia:

Caution water on road during rain.

SIGN in Italy:
Danger: Fall in water mind your children.

Tai Wo STATION, Hong Kong:

The toilets will be partially suspended for use.

In PHILADELPHIA'S Chinatown:
Please Open the Door Hardly

Spanish rental APARTMENT:

Deposit: The owner asks for a deposit of 25.000 ptas
as a guarantee for the flat.

This amount will be returned at the end of your stay if
any damage has been done.

SKI chalet, Nagano, Japan:
Let's skiing.

On seawall on Mediterranean coast of Italy, a warning sign that meant
"slippery shoreline" was translated SIMPLY as:
Area near the sea

Bus STATION, Laos:

Figure out fare office

Museum of the Revolution, HAVANA, Cuba:

The museum are making different constructions work.
Please we entreat excuse.

LISTED on a map in a park in Shanghai, China:

Pleasure grounds

Saldanha Bay, South AFRICA:

Warning!

To all seagulls swimming in red water is
strictly prohibited.

On a TRASH can in Amorgos, Greece:

Useless box

LOG FLUME ride, Europa Park amusement park, near Freiburg, Germany:

Do not leaning or reaching out of the boat is
stridly forbidden.

Be careful to butt head on wall.

Sign in Shanghai, CHINA:

Shanghai Citizen

"Seven Don't" Criterion

A. Don't expectoration everywhere

B. Don't chuck garbage everywhere

C. Don't attaint public property

D. Don't destroy virescence

E. Don't random through street

F. Don't smoking in public concourse

G. Don't say four-letter word

Liaocheng, CHINA:

Care the stairs.

NEXT to a bin in Wuhan, China:
Poisonous and evil rubbish

Plastic sign warning Japanese passers-by of ongoing work on electric CABLING:

Execution in progress

In a small town outside BEIJING, China:

Welcome to tourism holiday spot Hurauo and expect everything to turn out as you wish.

OUTSIDE a Japanese office block:

The most finest address

Resort at IGUACO FALLS on the border between Argentina and Paraguay:

We offer you peace and seclusion.

The paths to our resort are only passable by asses. Therefore, you will certainly feel at home here.

On trash CANS in Japan:

Trush

IN Greece:

Handycraft Studio's Exhibition of Disabled People

Sign on a house, PUERTO Rico:

Warning: Strange Dog

At Mallorca AIRPORT:

Distinguished Visitor: It is known that all the turistic services in Mallorca are maintaining a correct relation price quality, but even though, we wish to prize the establishments and services that to the opinion of our visitors, surpass notoriously for their quality.

To be able to fill out these questionnaires you must write the name of this establishment, installation or turistic service, as is shown below, and you must give a punctuation between 6 and 10 points hoping that the service that you must punctuate has been the best in the relation price-quality.

Florence, ITALY:

You are in a monumental palace, alike an Ufitzi's galley of Florence.

You are therefore kindly requested to behave consequently.

At a PARK in China:

Trees and flowers await your love.

TOURIST site in Beijing:

No fight, scrap, scrabble, rabble, feudal, fetish or sexy service.

Sign above a BUILDING under construction, Kyoto, Japan:

We're sorry but please expect.

Yudu SCENIC spot in China:

Please don't surpass the cautionary driftwood while having the aquatic visiting.

Kyoto IMPERIAL Palace, Japan:

If a tour group contains more than the number stiputed above, it is different in application.

The particulars will be asked the clerk at the window. A man below 18 years old should be accompanied by the adults.

- - - - - - - - - - - - - - - - - - ➤ Sign on a DOOR in Israel, meant to say "Staff only":

For stuff only

RULES for climbing Mount Fuji, Japan:

A teffific gust often overtakes three times consecutively. Keep yourself lying flat on the siope until it's completely blown over.

Danger comes soonest when it's despised.

In case of bad weather such as, storm, fain, snow and a dense fog, avoid climbing futher than the fifth staition. when the weather breaks suddely. just give up half-way and return.

The nearest-to-the-sky location in Japan is far colder than the feets of the mountain.

Bring garbage back to your home.

CASH machine in China:

Help oneself terminating machine.

China:

Notice of passerby:

Please maintain the hygienic conditions. Cherish the public property and no smoking. spit and garbage in the staircase.

Please don't resort and no pitchman.

Please contact with the manager in time If you have any difficulty.

Please take one step forward and crap twice.

A BANNER in Hong Kong meant to read "Don't Worry, Be Happy":

Don't Worry, Be Sammy

Sign on cash MACHINE in Paris:

Temporarily inalienable terminal. Please excuse us for the caused embarassment.

Information Complain the place

Some locations seem to possess a special genius for befuddled signs. Swimming pools, for instance . . .

HOTEL pool, Istanbul, Turkey:

No diving. No nakedness. No ruining.

---→ **France:**

Swimming is forbidden in the absence of the savior.

Eldorado, SANTA FE, New Mexico:

Violations will be enforced.

Plantation Bay resort, PHILIPPINES:

Swimming pool suggestions:

Open 24 hours.

Lifeguard on duty 8 a.m. to 8 p.m.

Drowning absolutely prohibited.

Sri LANKA:

Do not use the diving board when the swimming pool is empty.

ELEVATORS HAVE A SIMILAR TALENT . . .

LEIPZIG, Germany:

Do not enter the lift backwards, and only when lit up.

HOTEL in Tokyo, Japan:

Do not open door until door opens first.

Hotel in Belgrade, SERBIA:

To move the cabin, push button for wishing floor.

If the cabin should enter more persons, each one should press a number of wishing floor.

Driving is then going alphabetically by national order.

Let us know about an unficiency as well as leaking on the service.

Our utmost will improve it.

Tokyo:

Keep your hands away from unnecessary buttons for you.

ALSO ZOOS . . .

PHUKET, Thailand:

Common Wild Pig

Don't Eat The Animals

Budapest, HUNGARY:

Please do not feed the animals.

If you have any suitable food, give it to the guard on duty.

---► Japan:

Children found straying will be taken to the lion house.

CZECH Republic: ◄--------------------------------------

No smoothen the lion.

. . . and finally, the GREAT Wall of China:

The most magnificent strange stone city in China

Don't climb on the U-shaped opens.

At a zip-wire slide near the Great Wall, SIMATAI:

1. Those who suffer from high blood pressure, mental disease, horrifying of highness and liquour heads are refused.

2. Those who are above 65 years old and the disabled are refused.

3. Each set of belt for one person only. Hold tightly the belt when you are seated.

4. When you are using the belt, please follow the instruction of the staff. Never use only by yourself.

5. Take good care of your personal belongings to avoid the drop-off from your hand.

ROMANTIC RAMBLINGS

➡ That old devil called love has had us all in its spell at one time or another. Finding the right words to describe how we feel can be a challenge. For some people, it's a real challenge . . .

41, with 18 years of teaching in my behind.

Looking for American-born woman who speaks English very good.

Message on an INTERNET dating site, from a Thai woman to her prospective partner:

I started go aerobic dance, because I am fat.

I think, when you come Thailand, you want to see me on slim body!

Russian woman's lonely-hearts ADVERTISEMENT:

I am looking for an realy educated man who can be joke to himself.

SOMETIMES, WHOLE RELATIONSHIPS CAN GET A LITTLE MIXED UP . . .

Text message from an Italian BOYFRIEND to his English girlfriend:

Here is coldest. I need your familiar worm burning kisses.

Are you like spend your free time in contry or in town? shopping or walking on the hilly, or long the cost on the beach. or just seat look the landscape. I did like know more about you, that i try to make for you my best. let my know about you We had so little time (so nice), i would like spend more e more time with you I remember your eyes,(bellissimi) last things i was looked in you. Beautyfull memory.

He's still GOING:

Life is very peaky for me here but knowing that someone is on the other side of the sleeve sea is thinking on me makes me strong.

Now he's been to the DOCTOR and is suffering from . . . ◄ - - - - - - - - - - - - - - -

high blond pressure.

Things are TENSE between the Italian and his girlfriend. He suggests a tête-à-tête to resolve matters. Or rather, he suggests an . . .

air-cleaning vis a vis.

MISCELLANEOUS MUSINGS

→ Some of the things that get lost in translation not only defy understanding, they defy categorization . . .

Taiwanese poster PUBLICIZING Guinness World of Records exhibition:

In this kaleidoscopic world, nothing is too strange, extraordinary men and affairs, including all phenomena. Welcome to 'surprising world of Guinness World of Records Museum to enjoy the records' maintainers' live performances and world folk-custom show.

The slogan for Salem cigarettes is "Salem—Feeling Free." In JAPAN, this was translated as:

When smoking Salem, you will feel so refreshed that your mind seems to be free and empty.

Translation of "Permanent Under-Secretary" on Japanese business card:

Everlasting typist

PORTUGUESE patent agent:

It will not be necessary to state the name and address of the inventor if the applicant is not himself.

In 1855 PEDRO CAROLINO published The New Guide of the Conversation in Portuguese and English. Unfortunately, Carolino didn't actually speak any English—he wrote the book by referring to a Portuguese-French phrase book, then a French-English dictionary.

The "conversation" section included:

Apply you at the study during that you are young.

I am catched cold in the brain.

If can't please at everyone one's.

I dead myself in envy to see her.

This girl have a beauty edge.

Do no might one's understand to speak.

The vocabulary section included:	Defects of the Body:
Of the Man:	A blind
The brain	A lame
The brains	A bald
The fat of the leg	A left handed
The ham	An ugly
The inferior lip	A squint-eyed
The superior lip	A scurf
The entrails	A deaf
The reins	

President Heinrich Lubke, welcoming
QUEEN ELIZABETH II to West Germany in the 1960s:

Who are you?

On the same trip, at the THEATER (attempting to tell her that the
performance would begin any minute):

Equal goes it loose.

SEWAGE treatment plant, as marked on a Tokyo map:

Dirty Water Punishment Place

Advertisement in U.S. Asia Times for a PROFESSIONAL interpreter:

Are you unable to express your in English?

I can help you in the right earnest.

Translation agency's advertisement in the MOSCOW Times:

Bet us your letter of business translation do.

Every people in our staffing know English like the hand
of their back. Up to the minuet wisestreet phrases,
don't you know, old boy.

British soccer team slogan "You'll Never Walk Alone," as printed on a SHIRT in Liaocheng, China:

You'll Never Pickle Again

Madras (Chennai, India) newspaper:

Our editors are colleged and write like the Kipling and the Dickens.

Norwegian Prime MINISTER after a service in Brazil:

Thank you for the mess.

Newly APPOINTED Danish minister:

I am in the beginning of my period.

German-English TEXTBOOK:

After a certain time cheques are stale and cannot be cashed.

IN a Paris guidebook:

To call a broad from France, first dial OO.

Bring me a partion of . . .

Only half a partion of . . .

Smocking/No Smocking

Bring me, we are in a harry!

Greek flavourable sweets and candies

Chocolates: plain, milk, Pavlidoo, bitter

This is to go at deffered rate (halt rate).

I cannot speek.

mother—brother—sister—
ground father—ground mother . . .

ITALIAN reader's review of About a Boy by Nick Hornby: ◄-------------------

It is the perfect kind of reading for having some relax and enjoying one's own free time. Despite the subject of it might seem trivial, it provides indeed some interesting starting points for reflecting on some issues of our life, which often seem more troublesome of what they deserve to be.

Italian FURNITURE advertisement:

Big leather pieces only joint by an intangible stitching create a perfect balance of proportions.

CAIRO, Egypt, Internet café:

Please you are not allowed to enter or open the following sites: a, the sexual sites; b, religion sites; c, political sites. Thank you for your co-operator.

Russian chess BOOK:

A lot of water has been passed under the bridge since this variation has been played.

ADVERTISEMENT in an Indian newspaper:

For sale to kind master: Full grown tigress, goes daily walk untied, and eats flesh from hand.

From the SOVIET Weekly:

There will be a Moscow Exhibition of Arts by 15,000 Soviet Republic painters and sculptors. These were executed over the past two years.

Names of buildings in Bangkok, THAILAND:

TIT Tower and PMT Mansion

Exceuse me!

Are You Toilet Full?

If it full. We take out for you.

If not it. O.K.

Ask about our plans for owning your home.

On a Danish Web site for pesticides:

Pests: Trips constitutes only a small problem.

Use utility animals or insecticide soap.

Eventually showering with water.

Watering: Scarcely watering is recomended. Tolerates drying out periodes between watering.

No special demand to the housewive's green thumbs.

Taxi DRIVER in Cairo, trying to chat up English tourists:

Jubbly lovely.

FROM a Japanese newspaper article:

Four people were killed, one seriously.

International dormitory in KANSAI, Japan:

Do not bring the newspapers to your room.

It might disturb other residents.

An INVITATION to a picnic:

Join! You will meet strange people!

ADVERTISEMENT in Beijing, China:

Our watches are waterproof, shock-proof and time-proof.

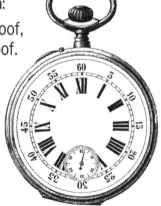

A thorough extermination of the building is presently necessary.

FROM the Montreal Gazette:

Ordinary People has been falling in popularity ever since Mary Tyler Moore's real life son committed death.

AT a Montreal club:

During the renovation of the main entrance, members should use the old ladies' entrance.

Card of "recommandation" for a MINIATURE golf course in Ostend, the Netherlands:

Level with the feet holes or mound do by playing on the game.

No working players are invited to stay on the stony mat.

On a T-SHIRT, Hong Kong:

Child be a public servant. The best balance of music and technology within a vaguely.

On a Japanese T-shirt:

Polygon Form: It is a solid image by the line and plane. Anyone is assembled on the screen.

- ➤

On a FRENCH pest-control firm's Web site:

Small animals nibble you the life?

They give you the cockroach?

Brochure for Odaiba, JAPAN:

Some people just think that Odaiba is just like a double sided magic mirror. Yes, exactly. Whatever dream you have, you may find its trace and realize it in Odaiba. Just tour through Odaiba by Free Shuttle Bus. To your surprise, you may make new friends.

East AFRICAN newspaper: ◄ - - -

A new swimming pool is rapidly taking shape since the contractors have thrown in the bulk of their workers.

Sign in the Netherlands advertising a Dutch-English GRAMMAR tutor:

Englisch as she is goodly pocken.

Shower of happiness.

Total safety guaranteed.

---→ **On a T-shirt in JAPAN:**

I lile the present situation very much.

Marketing flyer from a Spanish COMPANY:

Half statement of press publishes and distributes free sectors publications of the most representative Spanish industry in order to collaborating exporter of the products and manufactured of happiness in the expansion companies, for the one which we have considered you could be of their interest know to the detail the reference of the fabric industrial Spaniard, of the that they are facilitated the reasons social, complete adresses and description of the productive activity for medium from journalistic reports.

Brochure for an AMUSEMENT park in Odaiba:

In this real environment replicated entertainment park, you can enjoy the very things of Hongkong by just stepping your foot one step in. Here lies the amazing experience never elsewhere.

Taiwanese advertisement for a LAPTOP computer:

Take it to take off away from where other majority has stayed long since. Not only abreast it keeps you but also ahead of the cornfield of computing.

BROCHURE for Odayku Museum, Japan: ◄- -

There are a newspaper publishing company and a special exibition by own company plan.

Be planned a wide genre from a picture to a photograph by richness.

Brochure for Idemitsu MUSEUM, Japan:

Have formality of the first kabuki play ground.

There is the earphone guide who can hear explanation which enjoying the play.

ITALIAN marketing flyer:

This publication has dedicated the necklace of nature classical hybrid and is extensive in four tongues to scholastic custom, whose production, that to full rhythm will be of menstrual lilt, satisfies the Italian market, for which we retain, might fully interest

you it am because the commodity is economic.

I never use shampoo with milk or eggs.

These are imperialist ideas.

From a Japanese WEB site:

The contents of this website make service offer in Japan now.

The direction which does not understand Japanese well is this advanced ON prohibition.

Note left for a British visitor who had taken his Dutch hosts their favorite products, including loose tobacco:

Dear Pete,

Thank you for the chocolate, the coffee and the shag.

BUSINESS letter sent out when Götabanken changed its name to Gota Bank:

Dear friends,

We are the same guys as before, although we have lost our pricks.

JAPANESE graffiti:
FACK YOU MAN

Advertisement in Angling Times (UK MAGAZINE):
Executioner Pole, 13m, unused, used twice.

Résumé MISHAPS:

My intensity and focus are at inordinately high levels and my ability to complete projects on time is unspeakable.

Education: Curses in liberal arts, curses in computer science, curses in accounting.

Instrumental in ruining entire operation for a Midwest chain store.

I am a rabid typist.

Proven ability to track down and correct erors.

Strengths:

Ability to meet deadlines while maintaining composer.

I demand a salary commiserate with my extensive experience.

I have lurnt Word Perfect 6.0, computor and

spreadsheat progroms.

Received a plague for Salesperson of the Year.

Reason for leaving last job: maturity leave.

Personal interests:

Donating blood. Fourteen gallons so far.

Wholly responsible for two (2) failed financial institutions.

Failed bar exam with relatively high grades.

Let's meet, so you can ooh and aah over my experience.

You will want me to be Head Honcho in no time.

I Am a perfectionist and rarely if if ever forget details.

I am loyal to my employer at all costs.

Reason for leaving last job: They insisted that all employees get to work by 8:45 every morning.

Could not work under those conditions.

The company made me a scapegoat, just like my three previous employers.

Finished eighth in my class of ten.

And from a COVER letter:

Thank you for your consideration.

Hope to hear from you shorty!

Slogan on mugs produced by a BRITISH cricket club, who wanted to bill their star player "King of Spin":

Ashley Giles—King of Spain

From an eBay advertisement for a Chinese STAMP album:

Contains stamps on more than 30 different subjects, which are listed chronically in 20+ well printed thick pages.

AND FINALLY . . .

NAME of the author of this book, as listed on a Japanese Web site leading up to publication:

Charlie Crocker